History of the Parish of West or Old Kilpatrick and of the church and certain lands in the parish of East or New Kilpatrick. [With illustrations.]

John Scot Bruce

History of the Parish of West or Old Kilpatrick and of the church and certain lands in the parish of East or New Kilpatrick. [With illustrations.]
Bruce, John Scot
British Library, Historical Print Editions
British Library
1893
ix. 341 p. ; 8°.
10370.dd.26.

OR O

ATRIC

AND CERTAIN LANDS

OF EAST OR NEW

BY

JOHN BRUCE, F.S.A.

ILLUSTRATIONS AND

Glasgow:

& SON, 70 RENFIELD STREET

CONTENTS OF PART I.

CONTENTS OF PART II.

(To be issued shortly).

including amongst other Illustrations a drawing of the old Church of Kilpatrick by the late Miss Grace Hamilton of Cochno.

HISTORY OF THE PARISH

OF

WEST OR OLD

KILPATRICK

AND OF

THE CHURCH AND CERTAIN LANDS

IN THE PARISH OF EAST OR NEW KILPATRICK

BY

JOHN BRUCE, F.S.A. Scot.

LET KILPATRICK FLOURISH.

GLASGOW

JOHN SMITH & SON, Renfield Street

MDCCCXCIII

SLATER & LIDDELL,

PRINTERS,

133 WEST REGENT STREET,

GLASGOW.

INTRODUCTORY NOTE.

IN presenting this volume dealing with the history of my native parish, I hope that in spite of its manifest shortcomings it will meet with a sympathetic reception from those connected with or interested in the district. Due acknowledgment will be given in the concluding chapter of the willing and valuable assistance rendered by many kind friends, accompanied by a list of the various authorities from which much of the information engrossed in the following pages has been derived.

J. B.

HELENSBURGH,
8th August, 1893.

The Heliogravure Co.

Glasgow.

VIEW FROM DALNOTTER HILL, A.D. 1812.

From a Water Colour Painting by H. W. Williams.

WEST KILPATRICK.

GENERAL DESCRIPTION.

THE important parish of West or Old Kilpatrick, which derives its name from Saint Patrick, the tutelary Saint of Ireland, is situated in the old province of the Levenax or Lennox, and stretches along the north bank of the River Clyde from Yoker Burn in the east to Gruggie's Burn in the west, a distance of some 7¾ miles, its utmost breadth from north to south being 5½ miles. In shape it is not unlike a triangle, with the base towards the river. It is bounded on the north and east by the parishes of Killearn, East or New Kilpatrick, and Renfrew, and on the west and north-west by that of Dumbarton. Originally East or New Kilpatrick—or, as it was anciently called, Drumry parish—was embraced within the boundaries, but on 16th February, 1649, "in respect of the largenes of the parish and for the

better helping of the ministers' stipends," the Scottish
Parliament agreed to the division as proposed by the
Presbytery of Dumbarton.* In 1875, owing to the great
increase of the population, Duntocher—which had been
a *quoad sacra* charge from the year 1856—was consti-
tuted a parish *quoad omnia*, Clydebank being at same
time similarly disjoined.

The parish contains several lochs and sheets of water,
the largest of which are Loch Humphrey, in size 6 furlongs
by 3 furlongs, and Cochno Loch, 4 furlongs by ¾
furlongs; the latter is said to have been the trout preserve
for the Abbey of Paisley.

The scenery of the district—which is beautifully diversi-
fied—has long been admired, the view of the river and
mountains westward from Dalnottar being considered one
of the finest prospects on the Clyde. The scenery from that
point has long been a favourite subject with artists, and,
as early as the end of last century, Mr. Farringdon, Royal
Academician, London, a man of eminence in his profession,
was employed to take views on the rivers Forth and Clyde,
and that from Dalnottar Hill was supposed by many to
be the best in the collection.† This view, painted by
Naysmith, was the subject of the drop scene of the old
Theatre Royal, Queen Street, Glasgow, and it is said

* See Appendix A.
† Old Statistical Account, vol. v., Edinburgh, 1793.

£100 was offered and refused for it a few days before
the theatre was burned down.   At one time the road
from Glasgow led right over Dalnottar Hill, thus afford-
ing to travellers every opportunity of enjoying the scenery.
The following extracts from Stoddart's "Local Scenery
and Manners in Scotland,"* and Dibdin's "Tour in
Scotland,"† are of interest, as showing the favourable
impressions the scenery from this point produced on
cultured minds.

Stoddart writes—"Two or three miles further, you fall
into the Dumbarton road, which here crosses the canal,
and immediately begins to ascend Dalnottar Hill; on
reaching the top of which, near the house of ——
Davidson, Esq., a most beautiful view bursts upon you
at once.   On the left, in the vale below, flows the
Clyde, with the canal carried close along its banks.
On the opposite side of the river is Erskine, a well
wooded seat of Lord Blantyre's, the green points of
which, receding behind each other, form the head of
the Firth of Clyde; the river now swelling into an
estuary, and appearing like a noble lake shut in by the
bold and lofty Argyleshire mountains in the distance;
and immediately below you is the right bank of the
Clyde, ornamented by a continued succession of pleasant

* London, 1801, page 200.
† London, 1801, pages 180 and 181.

points, from the small village of Kilpatrick, to the town of Dumbarton, whose singular rock and castle already strike you with admiration. Upon the whole, the view from Dalnottar hill is not only remarkable, as being the first in this tour which presents an idea of the grandeur of Highland scenery, but as combining, in an eminent degree, many characteristics of the grand and beautiful.

"The approach of evening induced me to take up our night's lodging at a small public-house in Kilpatrick, where, as we did not expect very luxurious fare or very splendid accommodations, we were not disappointed."

While Dibdin writes—"We saw all at once the opening view from Dalnottar Hill, with Dumbuck, Dumbarton Rock, for the castle is at that place concealed, the winding Clyde, and the extensive distance beyond Port-Glasgow and Greenock, which formed altogether a most beautiful and striking effect. All other considerations became suspended; out came the pencil. At this time a light shower was passing off, which gave a pearly and sober appearance to the view, massing objects together and softening down all outlines." (The drawing referred to is in comparison with Williams,' which forms our frontispiece, a very crude production, the locality being barely recognisable.) "Having achieved this feat, we bade adieu to Dalnottar and its extensive ironworks, and came to Kilpatrick, where, according to tradition, was born the tutelary saint of Ireland."

Miss Dorothy Wordsworth, who travelled through Clydesdale in 1803, writes in glowing terms of the Dalnottar view. The frontispiece is from an engraving of a water-colour painting by H. W. Williams, known as "Grecian" Williams, dated 1812. The detail is remarkably faithful, showing many points which are still recognisable.

The view from the Kilpatrick Hills, which, with Dumbuck, form the most southerly spur of the Grampians, is unsurpassed for variety of scenery, comprehending as it does the rugged grandeur of the Highland mountains and the softer beauty of the fertile fields and valleys of the Lowlands. The highest points in the district are as follows, and are taken from the Ordnance Survey Map :—

Fynloch and Duncomb, ...	1,313 feet.
The Slacks, S.E. from Loch Humphrey,	1,199 ,,
Cochno Hill, ...	1,140 ,,
Lang Craig, ...	1,140 ,,
Loch Humphrey, ...	1,065 ,,
West Muirhouse Farm,* . . .	800 ,,
Hill of Dun, ...	681 ,,
Greenland Farm, ...	600 ,,
Dumbuck Hill, ...	547 ,,
Craigunnock, ...	515 ,,
Cochno Policies, ...	504 ,,
Ardconnel or Sheep Hill, Auchentorlie, .	500 ,,
Dumbowie Hill, ...	500 ,,

* Highest inhabited house.

Edenbarnet Road, ...	461 feet.
Dumbar Hill, ...	428 ,,
Blackmailing Farm, . . .	300 ,,
Carleith Farm, ...	207 ,,
Duntocher R.C. Chapel, ...	200 ,,
Drums, ...	200 ,,
Dunerbuck Farm, ...	180 ,,
Radnor Park, ...	150 ,,
N. E. Boquhanran or Chapel Yard, .	100 ,,
Gavinburn Farm, ...	80 ,,

The land naturally is well drained, but from the proximity of the hills to the river none of the streams are of great volume ; the most important being Duntocher Burn, which has its sources in Loch Humphrey and the adjoining slopes, and falls into the Clyde at Dalmuir.

The other streams are Yoker Burn ; Lusset Burn, Kilpatrick ; Auchentorlie Burn, Little Mill ; Milton Burn, and Gruggie's Burn, at the western boundary of the parish.

ROADS.—The parish is traversed from one end to the other by the highway leading from Glasgow to Dumbarton, and running parallel with the river. * About the year 1760 there were no passable roads for carriages owing to the want of bridges, for in floods the rivulets were unfordable. Ten years or so afterwards the Duke of Argyle, Lord Frederick Campbell, and Sir Archibald Edmonstone, one of the heritors of the parish, undertook

---

* Old Statistical Account, vol. v., page 220, Edinburgh, 1793.

to make part of the high road from Yoker to the
town of Dumbarton, a stretch of about 8 miles, and
to take the chance of the tolls for their indemnification,
which at the time was considered a very uncertain
security. The road was soon made in the completest
manner, and in 1793, through the increase of the trade
in the parish and the number of travellers, the turn-
pike dues had repaid the money advanced. Towards the
end of last century the road leading from Kilpatrick to
Duntocher and East Kilpatrick, which was the old highway
from Dumbarton to Stirling, was similarly improved, to
the great benefit of the parish.

Another and very old road, passing through the
Abbey lands, commences at Dalmuir, strikes northward
from the Dumbarton highway to where N.W. Boquhanran
Farm formerly stood, of which Mr. Walter M'Laren, now
of Carleith, was the last tenant. The farm-house has
had to make way for the villas erected there within the
last few years. The road then runs thence eastward past
N.E. Boquhanran or Chapel-yard, and on to Kilbowie,
Drumry, Drumchapel, and Garscadden. At all points
the parish is well intersected by roads kept in excellent
repair, the metal required being mainly supplied from
the whinstone quarry at Bowling.

In August, 1878, the Act to alter and amend the
law in regard to the maintenance and management of

roads and bridges in Scotland was passed, by which it was provided that 5 years afterwards, unless in the meantime the Act should be adopted, or tolls and statute labour be legally abolished in such county, the existing system should end. Accordingly on the 1st of June, 1883, the tolls and gates throughout the parish were discontinued, and the roads are now maintained by an equal assessment on landlord and tenant—on the landlord solely when he occupies his own house.

On the Dumbarton road the toll-houses and gates were at Yoker Burn, Dalmuir, and Glenarbuck Burn, Bowling. On the Duntocher road there was a check bar near the old Parochial Schoolhouse, Old Kilpatrick, and a toll-house at Law Muir and Canniesburn, New Kilpatrick.

CANAL.--The Forth and Clyde Canal, which has its western terminus at Bowling Bay, was, with great ceremony, declared open on 28th July, 1790. The *Scots' Magazine* for August thus describes this interesting event :—

" Glasgow, 30th July. The important event of opening the Forth and Clyde Canal or Navigation from sea to sea, took place on Wednesday, and was evidenced by the sailing of a track barge belonging to the company of proprietors, from the basin of the canal near Glasgow, to the River Clyde, at Bowling Bay. The committee of management, accompanied by the magistrates of Glasgow, were the first voyagers upon this new navigation. On the arrival of the vessel at Bowling Bay, and after descending from the last lock in the Clyde, the ceremony of the junction of the Forth and Clyde was performed in presence of a great crowd of spectators, by Archibald Speirs, Esq., of Elderslie, chairman of the committee of management, who, with the assistance of the chief engineer, Robert Whitworth, launched a hogshead of water of the River Forth into the Clyde, as a symbol of joining the eastern and western seas together."

The first vessel to pass through was the sloop "Agnes," of 80 tons burthen, belonging to Port-Glasgow, and built at Leith for the herring fishery and coasting trade. This took place on 31st August, 1790; on 9th September, the sloop, "Mary M'Ewan," was the first to accomplish the passage eastward.

The opening of the Great Canal was attended with very advantageous consequences to the parish, and indeed to the county at large. It is said the use of the wheel-barrow was unknown in the west of Scotland until introduced in the construction of the Canal. Formerly the removal of earth and stones was accomplished by two men carrying a hand-barrow. At the 1st January, 1791, the Canal Company had expended in this undertaking above £330,000, the aqueduct over the Kelvin alone having cost £8,509. The extreme length of the navigation from Lock No. 1, on the River Forth at Grangemouth, to Lock 39, on the Clyde, is 35 miles.

Summit of the head level, ...	156 feet.
Medium width of the surface of the canal, .	56 ,,
,, bottom ,, .	27 ,,

Depth throughout, ...	8 feet.	
Number of locks on the east, . . .	20	
,, west, . . .	19	
Length of the locks between the gates, .	74 feet.	
Width between the walls, ...	20 ,,	
Fall of each lock, ...	8 ,,	

The sandstone used in building the sea-locks at Bowling
Bay and many of the bridges upon the west end of
the canal was taken from Auchentoshan estate.*

The canal, when first constructed, being deeper than
the River Clyde the Liverpool traders, one particularly,
called the "Ariel," a brig-rigged vessel, went to Port-
Dundas and discharged her cargo there, not being
able on account of her draft to reach the Broomielaw.

RAILWAYS.—The first railway in the parish was that
from Balloch and Dumbarton, with its terminus at
Frisky Hall, Little Mill, where the passengers were
transferred to the river steamers. It was completed in
1850. The year 1858, however, was signalised by the
completion of the line from Glasgow to Helensburgh.
The line was opened for passenger and goods traffic on
Monday, the 31st May of that year, under the most
favourable auspices, the weather being very delightful.
There was no formal demonstration at the opening; all
the trains were largely patronised from both ends, as well

as at the intermediate stations, upwards of 200 passengers having left Helensburgh for Glasgow by the morning train. The transference of Messrs. J. & G. Thomson's shipbuilding yard to the Barns estate led to further railway extension, and on 1st December, 1882, the Yoker and Clydebank Railway was opened for traffic. The Lanarkshire and Dumbarton Railway Company, having obtained Parliamentary powers in 1892, are now constructing a railway which will prove a serious competitor to the existing Line, but it is hoped that both Companies will find the traffic in passengers and goods sufficiently remunerative.

As already mentioned, the River Clyde forms the southern boundary of the parish. During last century the magistrates of Glasgow made great efforts to deepen the river, and found the principal obstacle was the ford at Dumbuck. Mr. John Golborne, Chester, the engineer employed to improve the navigation, having measured the depth of water there, found it to be 2 feet at low tide; 14 feet opposite Dunglass Castle; 2 feet at Kilpatrick sands, and recommended the construction of a quay at Dunglass, where vessels of large burthen could be moored at quarter flood. This was in 1769. In 1770 an Act of Parliament was obtained to contract the river by jetties, and deepen it by dredging "between the lower end of Dumbuck Ford and the bridge of

Glasgow, so as there shall be 7 feet of water in every part of the said river at neap tides." Improvements were immediately carried out, and Mr. Golborne reported on the 8th August, 1781, that at Dumbuck Ford, "we had the pleasure to find no less than 14 feet."

The following extract from Pennant's "Tour in Scotland," 1770,* is interesting, from the description it gives of the method of deepening the river at this time :—

" Take boat at (Glasgow) the quay, and after a passage of four miles down the River Clyde, reach the little flying house of Mr. Golborne, now fixed up on the northern bank, commanding a most elegant view of part of the county of Renfrew, the opposite shore. After breakfast, survey the machines for deepening the river, which were then at work. They are called ploughs; are large, hollow cases, the back is of cast iron, the two ends of wood, the other side open. These are drawn across the river by means of capstans, placed on long, wooden frames or flats, and opposite to each other, near the banks of the river. Are drawn over empty, returned with the iron side downwards, which scrapes the bottom and brings up at every return a half a ton of gravel, depositing it upon the bank ; and thus 1,200 tons are cleared every day. Where the river is too wide, the shores are contracted by jetties."

Since then the river has been gradually deepened, but so recently as 1812 the "Comet," drawing only 4 feet, required to leave Glasgow and Greenock respectively at or near high water, to prevent it grounding in the river. The late Mr. Thomas Macgill, shipbuilder, who died in 1882, could remember seeing the "Comet" lie ebbed off

Frisky Hall. On one occasion a disturbance having arisen among the passengers, a couple of the most obstreperous were quietly put over the side and allowed to wade ashore. Even in 1820 the sloop "John," of Bowling, drawing 5 feet, grounded on the Yoker sands, when going up the river.

In his book on the Clyde, Mr. James Deas, C.E., engineer to the Clyde Navigation, gives some curious information regarding the effect of the deepening, widening, and straightening of the river on the tides. In 1755 the Clyde at Glasgow was only 15 inches deep at low water, and 3 feet 8 inches at high water; thus giving a range of tide of only 2 feet 5 inches. It is now 15 feet deep at low water (writing in 1883), and 26 feet at high water; giving a tidal range of 11 feet. High water level has risen 9 inches since 1853, and low water level has fallen 23 inches within the same period, and 7 feet 10 inches since 1755. In 1800 the time of high water was three hours behind Port-Glasgow; now it is only one hour.

The deepening and straightening, as well as the embanking of the river has had a beneficial effect in preventing the overflow of the banks which used to take place after the prevalence of southerly winds, indeed so high were the tides that at times the Glasgow road between Yoker and Dalmuir was rendered impassable,

The launching of the "Comet" from the building yard of Messrs. John & Charles Wood, of Port-Glasgow, in June, 1812, was an event the successful results of which have tended in course of time to add materially to the commercial prosperity of the parish. Her dimensions were—40 feet keel, 10 feet 6 inches beam, and 25 tons burthen. In the *Greenock Advertiser* of 15th August, 1812, the following advertisement appears:—

STEAM PASSAGE BOAT,

THE COMET,

CAPTAIN WILLIAM MACKENZIE,

Between Glasgow, Greenock, and Helensburgh,

FOR PASSENGERS ONLY.

THE Subscriber having, at much expense, fitted up a handsome Vessel to ply upon the RIVER CLYDE, between GLASGOW and GRENOCK—to sail by the power of Wind, Air, and Steam—he intends that the Vessel shall leave the BROOMIELAW on TUESDAYS, THURSDAYS, and SATURDAYS, about Mid-day, or at such hour thereafter as may answer from the state of the Tide; and to leave Greenock on MONDAYS, WEDNESDAYS, and FRIDAYS, in the Morning, to suit the Tide.

The elegance, comfort, safety, and speed of this Vessel, require only to be proved to meet the approbation of the Public; and the Proprietor is determined to do everything in his power to merit public encouragement.

The Terms are, for the present, fixed at 4s. for the best Cabin, and 3s. the second; but beyond these rates nothing is to be allowed to servants, or any other person employed about the Vessel.

The Subscriber continues his Establishment at HELENSBURGH BATHS, the same as for years past; and a Vessel will be in readiness to convey Passengers in the COMET from Greenock to Helensburgh.

Passengers by the COMET will receive information of the Hours of Sailing, by applying at Mr HOUSTON'S OFFICE, Broomielaw; or Mr THOMAS BLACKNEY'S, East Quay Head, Greenock.

HENRY BELL.

HELENSBURGH BATHS,
5th August, 1812.

The excitement along the banks of the Clyde when the "Comet" first voyaged down the river was very

great, all the country side crowding down to see the wonderful craft propelled by the "power of wind, air, and steam."

Prior to the introduction of steamers on the Clyde, the principal means of communication between Greenock and Glasgow, and the various places on the banks of the river, was by the fly-boats, which were constructed by William Nicol, of Greenock. They were about 28 feet keel, from $7\frac{1}{2}$ to 8 feet beam, about 8 tons burthen, and wherry-rigged, and were, on the whole, well fitted up for passengers.

The boats generally started from Greenock with the first of the tide. If, however, wind and tide were adverse, which was frequently enough the case, no little labour was required with sails and oars to make any advance whatever, and both passengers and crew in such

untoward circumstances were often right glad on getting as
far up as Dunglass, to rest there for five or six hours till
the next tide should favour their further progress, ex-
changing meanwhile, their irksome confinement for a
ramble in the neighbouring woods, which in those days
were extensive, and, in the season, afforded excellent
nutting.

Sheriff Barclay, in his "Reminiscences of Glasgow,"* says
with reference to this detention: " It was surmised that
the 'flies' were intercepted there by a net or web in the
shape of a tavern.   The passengers had frequently to
remain in their ark or get quarters in the 'public' until
the morning's tide called them to resume their voyage.
A story was told and vouched, that when a 'fly' had
been thus arrested for the night, and the crew were
called in the early and dusky morn to avail themselves
of the favourable tide, the two boatmen, who had been
meantime indulging in strong drink, set to work with
their oars.   With the dawn the passengers had a dreamy
notion that they were making little or no progress, as
the outline of the castellated rock still, phantom-like,
appeared in the mist.   Calling the attention of the
rowers to their apprehensions, the fact was painfully
realised by the following colloquy between the ancient
mariners:- 'Tonald, did you lift t'anchor?' and the

---

* Glasgow, 1880, p. 176.

discouraging reply, 'Na, Tougal, not me, but 'twas your tudy.'"

FERRIES.—Erskine Ferry, which still remains, was the principal passage across the Clyde. At one time the portage was at Ferrydyke, immediately under the terminal Roman fort at Chapelhill, from which the compound name, Ferrydyke, is derived, but a sandbank having formed in the river early last century, the ferry was removed up to its present position. There was a ferry at Dunglass later, and also at Bowling canal sea-lock. The former was withdrawn when the wharf at Frisky Hall was built, and the latter when the upper wharf, now dismantled, was erected for the benefit of the Glasgowegians who patronised the Sutherland Arms Hotel. At Dalmuir there was a ferry-boat, the last tacksman being the late John Walker, a worthy elder in the United Presbyterian Church, Old Kilpatrick.

CHAPTER II.

PREHISTORIC REMAINS.

THE recorded prehistoric remains are, all things considered, very few in number. This may be accounted for by the fact that the lands of the district have been so long under cultivation, and that during a period when the study of archæology had practically no existence.

The deepening of the Clyde has led to several important discoveries of the craft in which our forefathers sailed and fished.

In 1854 the largest canoe hitherto recorded as excavated in the Clyde valley was discovered at Erskine Ferry by Mr. Gilbert Taylor, the tacksman of the ferry, and placed for inspection in the ferry-house garden. It was 33 feet in length, 4 feet in breadth, and of a depth of 3 feet 6 inches. The stern was flat and sloping, and the boards of oak fitted in a groove. The gunwale showed the appearance of iron locks on each side near the stern, and, judging from the distance between them, it would appear the craft had been propelled by 5 or 6 oars on each side. A visitor to Erskine Ferry, in 1856, records the almost entire disappearance of the canoe, it having been carried off in pieces by the curious. Some time later, about 1863, on the north side of the river, nearly opposite Renfrew, two canoes were laid bare, one of them being about 25 feet in length. In this connection it may be interesting to observe that the bones of a whale were discovered near Erskine Ferry in the year 1855. In 1868, in the river bend eastward from Dunglass Castle, Mr. Currie, then manager of the Little Mill Distillery, was instrumental in getting two canoes taken out of the river. They lay abreast of each other about two yards apart, their prows turned toward the south-west in a deposit of clay and sand. The larger canoe, composed merely of an undressed cylindrical hollow oak tree, of most uncouth aspect, measured 23½ feet in extreme length, and 11 feet in mean girth. Both ends had a truncated appearance, that which represented the prow having on the bottom side a formidable projection 2 feet in length, with a circular vertical perforation by which it might possibly be made fast to its moorings. The interior was well finished, being smoothed and carefully rounded, and capacious enough to have afforded room for 8 or 10 men. The lesser canoe measured 13 feet in length, 3 feet in breadth, and 2 feet in depth. It was neatly constructed, carefully finished, and must have originally been a tidy little craft. The sides had been fitted for row locks, and

two unmistakeable foot-rests were in the bottom near the
stern.   A club was found lying in the bottom of the

canoe, similar in shape to the "pettle," which was
in use up to the latest date by the local fishermen
for stunning the newly caught salmon.   These two
canoes lay in a specially constructed shed at the distillery for many years; thereafter they were removed to
the Kibble Palace, Botanic Gardens, Glasgow.   In the
same year a canoe, 22 feet long, was found a little
below Milton Island, near Dunglass, in which it is said
there were six stone axes, an oaken club, and a piece
of deer's antler.

According to local report there are one or two canoes
lying silted up on the Erskine shore opposite Bowling,
it being the case that, many years ago, what was considered to be an inverted canoe, was partially laid bare
there for some time.

In 1850 two unperforated spherical stones—one made
of highly polished red granite, a species of rock unknown
in the district—were shown to the late Sir Daniel Wilson,
author of the "Prehistoric Annals of Scotland," as part
of the contents of a cist, then recently opened in the

course of farming operations on the estate of Cochno.

At New Kilpatrick, some years ago, a hammer of coarse-grained dolerite was found. It is 9⅝ inches in length, 4⅜ inches in maximum width, and 3½ inches in thickness. It is now in Kelvingrove Museum.

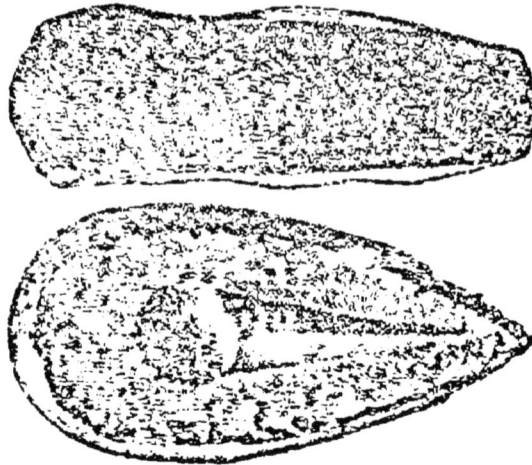

STONE HAMMER.

On the farm of Dawsholm, near Garscube, a barrow or tumulus was discovered about the year 1833, and in part opened up. Hitherto this mound, though sufficiently artificial, had attracted little observation, the curiosity of any chance inquirer being satisfied by the traditionary information of its being a court hill—one of those eminences on which Courts of Justice were held in the days of feudal jurisdiction. But the farmer, partly with the view of clearing his field of an incumbrance, and partly of obtaining soil to topdress other fields, set about removing the mound, and had not proceeded far in his

operations when he came upon a narrow flight of steps
leading upwards from the level of the field, not to
the centre of the tumulus, but towards a point in the
radius, distant about one-third of its length from the
outer extremity. This stair being followed six or seven
paces inward was found to terminate in a flagstone, on
which some ashes and cinders lay, and which emitted a
hollow sound on being struck with the tools of the
workmen. It was removed, and beneath it was discovered a narrow oblong trough or cell, walled with stone
on every side. In this several fragments of armour were
found, among which were apparently the visor of a helmet,
the head of a spear, and the blade of a sword, the first
being of copper, and the last of iron. Besides these,
there were what may have been a spade or shovel, much
turned up at the edges, two picks of a small size, and
several other articles, the purpose of which has not been
guessed—all of iron. There were no bones discovered,
and the stonework seemed to extend no further than has
been described.*

A most interesting discovery was made in the year
1887, by the Rev. Mr. Harvey, Duntocher, of cup and
ring markings on a rock surface, on the moor south of
Cochno House, in a field of furze and bracken, known
by the name of Craigpark, being the first of the kind

---

* New Statistical Account, vol. viii., page 36. Edinburgh, 1845

discovered in Dumbartonshire. The rock is composed of the hard sandstone of the district, and dips westward for about 60 feet. There is a group of four series of concentric circles united by radial grooves. The most easterly series consists of seven perfect rings round a central cup, and the radius of the outmost ring measures 18 inches. From the innermost circle of the first moves

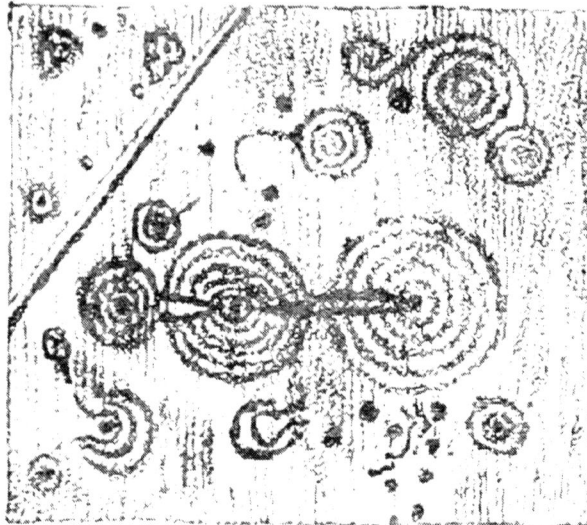

GROUP OF CUP AND RING MARKINGS

a duct, which passes to the innermost circle of the second, and is carried on to the outermost circle of the third. The second deviates from a circular to a rhomboidal appearance, with the same number of rings, but only a radius of 15 inches at the outside; and the third has five rings with no radial grooves and $8\frac{1}{2}$ inches for its

greatest diameter. Sometimes there is a duct, oftener
not, and it seems to have been cut both before and after
the rings had been formed. An interesting feature occurs
in a few with spiral volutes extending from the outermost
circle, and with three cups enclosed by one ring.
Numerous cups are distributed over this rock surface,

COCHNO HILL CUP-AND-RING SCULPTURINGS

and some of them are from 3 to 4 inches in diameter,
and from 2 to 2½ inches deep. These sculpturings are
said to be much richer than usual.

Following the Cochno rock sculpturings, in the year

in a dyke near the old farmhouse of Auchentorlie while the reservoir for the district water supply was being excavated close by. The sketches of both the Cochno and Auchentorlie sculptures are taken from the *Illustrated London News.*

In the spring of this year, 1893, a portion of a stone axe was found on the hill behind Carleith farm; and some cup and ring markings have been recently discovered by Mr. William Smith, Post Office, Duntocher, on a rock surface a short distance east from the same farm steading. Lord Blantyre has a bronze hatchet, picked up on the shore of the Clyde near Kilpatrick. (See Appendix B.)

CHAPTER III.

ROMAN REMAINS

ON the approach of the summer of the year A.D. 80, Agricola marched into Scotland to push his conquests further north. Having penetrated into the country as far north as the Tay, and having surveyed the district extending between the Clyde and Forth, he employed his troops in completing a series of detached forts across the isthmus at intervals of from two to three miles, from Old Kilpatrick in the west to the shores of the Forth near Borrowstoness.

On the departure of Agricola, the Romans immediately lost much of what they had gained in Scotland through the indecision and inaction of the Lieutenants who were appointed his successors. In the year 120, the Emperor Hadrian, who had ascended the Imperial Throne A.D. 117, visited this island and erected a wall of defence between the river Tyne and the Solway Firth. Soon after this he was obliged to take his departure in consequence of some disturbance which had occurred in Egypt.

On the decease of Hadrian A.D. 138, Titus Antoninus succeeded to the Imperial purple, and soon after appointed Lollius Urbicus as his Lieutenant in Britain, the rapidity of whose conquests was such that in the year 140 he had taken re-possession of the country as far as the estuaries of the Forth and Clyde, and proceeded at once to retain and strengthen the detached forts left by Agricola, and to unite them by one continuous wall. This great work consisted of a large rampart of sods of turf, or *murus cespiticius*, and must have originally measured about 12 feet in height and 14 feet in breadth at the base, which is of stone with squared kerbs. It was surmounted by a parapet having a level platform behind it for the protection of its defenders. In the front there extended along its whole course an immense fosse averaging about 40 feet wide and 20 feet deep, and to the southward of the whole was a military road from 18 to 24 feet wide. The construction of this rampart was assigned to detachments of the three legions, the II., VI. and XX., the permanent Roman Guard of Britain. In spite of the wall, in the year 180 the Caledonians again forced their way southward, and were driven back later by the Roman soldiers. In the year A.D. 208 the aged Emperor Severus, determined to crush the bitter hostility of the Northern Britons, marched northwards with an immense force, but after concluding a treaty with the natives and losing 50,000 men in the expedition, returned with the remains of his army to the south of the Tyne.

Constantine the Great, who died in 337, is said to
have so reduced the Caledonians, now called Picts, as to
deprive them of the means of giving him any further
annoyance.   In 367, Theodosius came northwards, and
after a series of victories again drove them beyond the
wall of Antoninus, over which they had some time before
made another incursion.

Early in the 5th century the Romans withdrew, and
the knowledge of their departure became a signal of
attack to the Scots and Picts, on the territories hitherto
protected by them.

The Roman remains in this parish are of first import-
ance, and I shall now proceed to describe these, and also
refer to the various descriptions of the traces of the wall
and remains as narrated in the works of those antiquarians
and travellers who, last century, bestowed much learning
and care on the subject.   At this day the traces of the
wall and ditch eastward to the farthest side of New Kilpatrick are few; in fact, to the casual observer the
remains to the west of Duntocher may be said to be
obliterated, but to the east, faint traces can be discerned
at Cleddan burn, and at the Castle hill further east, in a
wood there, the wall and ditch is in a fair state of preservation.   The numerous houses at East Kilpatrick recently built has led to the almost total destruction of
what was one of the best preserved portions of the vallum.

At Duntocher a section of the military way was laid bare recently, on the erection of the manse near the bridge.

From a very early date we find travellers carefully surveying the parish for traces of the Roman occupation, the first we read of being Dr. Irvine, who in 1686 was appointed historiographer royal of Scotland, and who travelled along the wall several times. As quoted by Sir Robert Sibbald, Dr. Irvine was of the opinion the wall began at Dumbarton, and states in his papers the following results of his investigations :—(1) At Dumbarton a great fort, (2) the Castle half a mile from it, (3) a mile thence at the foot of Dumbuck Hill a fort, (4) a mile thence at Dunglass a fort, (5) a mile thence to Chapelhill above the town of Kilpatrick a fort, and so on. Maitland, an acute and intelligent observer, the author of a History of Scotland, published in 1757, personally inspected the various places or forts referred to by Dr. Irvine, and says—"After the strictest search and inquiry, I could not learn that there was a fort at Dumbarton, and as to the fort at Dumbarton Castle it is only vestigia of certain trenches opened against the said Castle the last time it was besieged ; and the fort said to be at Dumbuck Hill seems rather to be the vestiges of an irregular sheepfold, and at Dunglass there is not the least appearance of a Roman work. That which has chiefly occasioned people

to be of opinion that the wall ran to Dunglass is a small
spot of ground at a place called the Dyke, about the length
of 40 feet by 4 feet by 2 feet deep, representing part of
a ditch, and from which the house* before it is denomi-
nated the Dyke, therefore it must have been part of the
trench belonging to the Roman wall, whereas by its
partly lying in and at the side of a garden, I take it to
be part of a ditch formerly appertaining to a garden.
Besides, as this small piece of trench is within a few feet
of the flood mark in the estuary of the Clyde, there is
not space left for the wall to have stood on, without
mentioning the military way that would have lain within
the same."

Bishop Pococke, who travelled in Scotland in 1760,
had the supposed traces of the wall at Bowling Bay,
referred to by Maitland, pointed out to him. In his
journal he says:—"On inquiry here (at Dunglass) about
the Roman wall, they showed me a mound in a garden,
which they said they took to be part of it, and that a
little further at a channel for water from the hill (Glenarbuck Burn), which is made under the road, they found
part of the field very stony, which they thought was
part of the foundation of the wall."

Maitland further says:—"That the Roman wall afore-

* This house stands on the north side of the road nearly opposite the
Buchanan Institute, Bowling.

said began at Kinneil in the east and ended where the village called the Ferry Dyke is at present situated, about a furlong bewest the town of Old Kilpatrick, appears by a tradition amongst the people, which is confirmed by the great number of Roman antiquities found there, and as an additional proof that the wall came to this place, we have the word Dyke, the latter part of the compound Ferry Dyke, after the same manner as the whole fence is called Graham's Dyke,* and as this seems to have been one of the most considerable or principal stations on the wall, I am of opinion that the Roman trajectus or ferry across the Clyde was at this place, as was of late the Old Kilpatrick ferry, but within these few years a sand-bank being arisen in the river, the ferry was removed a quarter mile higher up; and that nothing may be wanting to show that the wall ended at this place, I shall only add another tradition that the wall in its way thither ran along where the church of Old Kilpatrick is at present situated."

Horsely,† in discussing this subject, says :—"The common opinion and tradition of the people is in favour of the wall terminating at Dunglass. They talk of striking sometimes upon the foundation of the Roman wall at

---

* Or Grimes Dyke.
† "Britannia Romana."

the Close not half a mile north-east from Old Kilpatrick,
and then if the wall has proceeded in nearly the same
line, it must have gone as far as Dunglass before it
reaches the Firth. At Dunglass there is a fort, and the
lands juts out into the Firth, which is deep here close
to the shore; whereas near Old Kilpatrick the bottom is
flat and the river shallow, so that at low water there
would be room enough to pass by the end of the wall.
Besides, the military way has certainly been continued as
far as Dunglass, for it is very visible at Dunnerbuck.*
This at least makes it evident that there has been a
station there, whether we suppose the wall to have been
so far continued or not. The principal arguments against
the opinion of the wall being continued so far as Dunglass are these: that there are no visible remains of it
further west than Old Kilpatrick, the seeming faint appearance of the ditch near Dunnerbuck not being such
as can be depended on, and that the mountains on the
north side along the skirts of which it must have been
carried on to Dunglass would render the continuation of
it almost entirely useless."

All authorities, inclusive of Gordon and General Roy,
who minutely surveyed the district in the years 1724
and 1755 respectively, agree that the traces of the Roman

* The track across the field below Glenarbuck House, running parallel with
the Dumbarton Road, referred to by both Maitland and Bishop Pococke.

PLATE I.

1

2

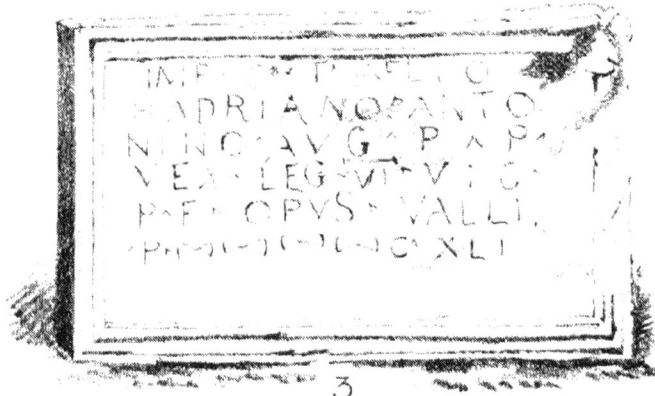

3

occupation begins at the Chapel Hill * or Ferry Dyke, lying midway between Bowling and Kilpatrick and from thence eastward.

Two tabular stones were found on the Chapel Hill, and presented to the University of Glasgow, by Mr. Hamilton, of Orbiston, in the year 1695. Both bear legionary inscriptions, one of which is as follows (Fig. No. 3, Plate I.):—

IMP · C · T · AELIO	IMPERATORI CAESARI TITO AELIO
HADRIANO · ANTO	HADRIANO ANTONINO
NINO · AVG · P · P ·	AUGUSTO, PATRI PATRIAE
VEX · LEG · VI · VIC ·	VEXILLATIO LEGIONIS SEXTAE VICTRICIS
P. F · OPVS · VALLI	PERFECIT† OPUS VALLI (PER)
P ∞ ∞ ∞ ∞ CXLI	PASSUS, QUATOUR MILLE CENTUM
	QUADRAGINTA UNUM

Announcing that the "Vexillation" of the sixth legion, surnamed "the Victorious," erected the said tablet in honour of the Emperor Titus Aelius Hadrianus Antoninus, the father of his country, having accomplished, in the formation of the wall, a portion of work to the extent of 4141 paces. A part of the other stone has been broken off and lost, but there is no difficulty in supplying the deficiency excepting the numerals which had preceded DXI in the concluding line. The interpretation is

* It is difficult to say how the name Chapel Hill has arisen, although the derivation perfectly obvious. There is a Chapel Hill on Hadrian's wall, where the remains of of a heathen place of worship have been discovered. Careful excavations might lead to a solution of the problem.

† Stuart suggests that instead of "carried on," as translated by Gordon, might it not rather read " perfected " or " finished."

similar to the former, with this difference, that the twentieth legion did the work instead of the sixth, and the fragmentary record of 511 paces of work completed. (Fig. No. 2, Plate I.). These inscriptions are engraved on slabs of common freestone.

Another stone, however, of much more artistic character, was likewise dug up on the Chapel Hill, and presented to the College of Glasgow by the Marquis of Montrose some time about the year 1695. This stone lay at Mugdock for some time (Fig. No. 1, Plate I.).

Stuart describes it as follows:—"There, within what may be called the mimic facade of a Corinthian portico, may be perceived the not inelegant form of a winged Victory, reclining with her left arm upon that emblem of empire, a globe; while in the one hand she holds a palm branch, and with the other points to, or rather touches, an oaken wreath— the well-known *Corona Civica,* or Civic Crown. Within this wreath appears conspicuous the name of the twentieth legion, the "Valiant and Victorious," while crowding the tympanum of the pediment above, are inscribed the usual names and titles of the Emperor Antoninus. On the pedestal may be observed the figure of a wild boar, apparently escaping, as if he heard the shouts of the Damnian huntsman in pursuit, his course lying between the two divisions of the line, which records the number of paces accomplished in the

formation of the wall. Instead of the peculiar figures
formerly made use of, the miliary mark seems to be
indicated in this instance by a transverse line which
crosses above the four I's on the left side of the pedestal.
Subjoined is a copy of the inscription, freed from the
contractions, and accompanied by a literal translation :—

IMPERATORI CAESARI
TITO AELIO HADRIANO
ANTONINO AUGUSTO PIO,
PATRI PATRIAE

To the Emperor Cæsar Titus Aelius
Hadrianus Antoninus Augustus Pius,
the father of his country.

VEXILLATIO LEGIONIS
VICESIMAE VALENTIS
VICTRICIS FECIT

The Vexillation of the Twentieth
Legion, (surnamed) the Valiant and
Victorious, performed

PER PASSUS, QUATOUR
MILLE QUADRINGENTOS
UNDECIM.

Four thousand four hundred and
eleven paces.

Maitland, already quoted, says, after describing the above
stone :—"Another stone I saw lying at the threshold
of the door of the most eastern house of Ferrydyke, of
28 inches square, and 6 inches thick, had a border of
3½ inches, curiously wrought, but the inner part being
greatly worn by people treading thereon, I could only
discern there had been an inscription there, which was
then unintelligible. This stone, which was dug up at
the eastward of the house where it lies, I take by its
form to have been a legionary stone erected in the wall
at or near the place where it was found, setting forth the

name of the legion and other particulars." He further
remarks—"There are many others of the same nation
built in the walls of the houses of Old Kilpatrick and
park walls in the neighbourhood."

In the year 1790, when the canal was being dug at
the south end of the Sufield Park, between Portpatrick
and the Ferrydyke drawbridge, a building constructed of
freestone and lime was unearthed. In the inside were
a considerable number of partitions about two feet apart,
archedover with bricks about 9 inches long, and as many
broad, while on the top of the arch were placed flat bricks
about 1½ inches thick, and of the same size. Inside
the building several rows of urns were found about 2 feet
deep and a foot and a half wide at the mouth, and
made of burnt clay, and in them a number of silver
coins were found covered over with earth. The writer [*]
of this account then goes on to say:—"Mr. Davidson, then minister, and Sir Archibald Edmondstone, who
was staying at the manse, got a number of the coins, as
did also Mr. Colquhoun, superintendent of the canal. I
got one of them which I gave to my uncle, the celebrated
John Knox, [†] which he told me afterwards was deposited
by him with the Scots' Antiquarian Society, London."
Stuart mentions, in 1844, that several denarii of Trajan
had then recently been found at the Chapelhill.

[*] MSS. John Millar Morrison.   [†] See page 39.

These are all the recorded remains found in the
vicinity of Kilpatrick, and it lies now with the Kilpatrick
Naturalist and Antiquarian Society to prosecute an
intelligent and diligent search by means of well considered
excavations for further objects connected with the Roman
occupation.

Eastward from Chapelhill or Ferrydyke, no trace of the
wall has been found until beyond the village of Kilpatrick, and on the east side of Sandyford or Lusset
Burn.

On the upper part of Sandyburn Hill, or North Dalnottar, * Maitland, and also General Roy, found traces
of the ditch, and Maitland remarks that at this place
the line of the wall points directly towards Ferrydyke. Between Carleith, on the north, and the Gateside
of Auchentoshan on the south, both Gordon and
Maitland found the ditch in great perfection, the
public road to Duntocher being evidently on the line of
the causeway or *via Militaris*. Horsely says that near
Gateside, and about 3 chains north from the wall, was
a small tumulus, and a pond, which, when drained
by Mr. Buchanan, the owner of the estate, was found
to be lined with hewn stones, and Mr. Buchanan was
of opinion it had been a Roman bath. At Auchentoshan,
an earthen vase and part of a stone bust were dug up,

---

* Formerly called by the country people Tittle Bog farm.

which seem entitled to claim a Roman origin ; the latter
resembles that of a Roman soldier, accoutred in his
cuirass (Fig. No. 4, Plate IV.). A fibula of bronze,
evidently Roman, in which were set some pieces of
coloured glass, was discovered on this section. Close
to Duntocher, Maitland found a few houses named the
Dyke, so called (in this instance correctly) from being
built on the wall, and also faint traces of the ditch to
the north. Passing on eastward the wall crossed
Duntocher burn to the north of the mill, and the
military way to the south, and thence up the hill to
the point known as the Golden Hill, on which was
situated Duntocher Fort.

The so-called Roman bridge at the Duntocher mill
was originally 8 feet wide ; but, in 1772, Lord Blantyre
made an addition of 6 feet to its width, as recorded
on the memorial stone standing hard by. Maitland is
of opinion that the original bridge was of wood, as the
rock underneath has evidently been cut to receive beams
of considerable thickness. The bridges of Hadrian's
Wall were thus constructed. Stuart is inclined to think
the bridge was built during the reign of King Robert
the Bruce while he resided at Cardross ; but, on the
other hand, I would venture to suggest that the architects
may have been the monks of Paisley Abbey, who thirled
their numerous tenantry in the parish to the Duntocher

Mill adjoining. General Roy, in his "Military Antiquities," gives a view of this bridge.

In 1778, some fine fragments of Roman pottery were brought to light. They were of red colour, glazed on both sides, and in excellent preservation. The best specimen among them represents two centaurs at a gallop, with the figure of an armed soldier standing under a canopy between them. Another is ornamented by a succession of circles like small shields, with a female figure in the centre of each, and a row of dolphins gamboling underneath. A third, which seems part of the rim of a barn, has the words BRVSC. F., supposed to be the maker's name—Bruscus Fecit—stamped upon it. A bar of lead, covered with rust, has also been discovered in the neighbourhood of Duntocher.

A London Scot, John Knox by name, whose father was a vintner in Kilpatrick, published a book of travels in 1785, entitled "Knox's View of Scotland." In Vol. II., fol. 611, he writes :—" Upon the declivity of the Golden Hill, in the vicinity of the bridge, in the year 1775, a countryman, in digging a trench, turned up several tiles of uncommon form. The tiles were of seven different sizes, the smallest being seven, and the largest twenty-one inches square. They were from two to three inches in thickness, of a reddish colour, and in perfectly sound condition. The lesser ones composed

several rows of pillars, which formed a labyrinth of passages of about 18 inches high, and the same in width, the largest tiles being laid over these pillars, served as a roof to support the earth on the surface, which was two feet deep, and had been ploughed through from time immemorial. The building was surrounded by a subterranean wall of hewn stone. Some professors in the University of Glasgow, and other gentlemen, having unroofed the whole, discovered the appearance of a Roman hot bath. The passages formed by rows of pillars were strewed with bones and teeth of animals, and a sooty kind of earth; in the bath was placed the figure of a woman, cut in stone, which, with a set of tiles and other curiosities found in this place, is deposited in the University." Knox remarks that he was returning from the Highlands when the discovery was made, and that, with threats and promises, he restrained the country people from demolishing the structure until it had been examined by those interested in such remains. He also says:—
"On the summit of the hill stood the Roman fort or castella. The foundation was lately erased by a clerk or overseer of an iron factory in the neighbourhood, who was, however, disappointed in his expectation of finding treasure. The same Goth expressed a strong desire to erase a fine remain of the Roman *via* which is carried along the base of the hill; but he hath not succeeded in his wishes, and

it rests with the family of Blantyre to prevent such practices in future upon the grounds of which they are superiors."

General Roy gives the dimensions of this fort at about 450 by 300 feet, measuring within the area of the ramparts, which, however, were so much dilapidated that the actual size and shape could with difficulty be ascertained. According to Gordon, one of the best executed legionary stones he had seen of all the Roman inscriptions discovered in Scotland was dug up at Duntocher some 160 years ago, and stood over the gateway of Cochno House, until Mr. Hamilton presented it to the University of Glasgow, where it now lies. (Fig. No. 3, Plate II.)

Stuart makes the following remarks on this particular piece of sculpture :—"On looking at it we might well be inclined to ask whence came the artist who rejoiced in the patronage of the Legio Secunda Augusta? In what region of the globe did he acquire the style displayed before us—original though rude—and what can be the meaning which his emblems bear? The present is but one specimen among many—all so much alike that we must either suppose some individual employé to have been an indefatigable workman, or else there existed a widespread partiality among the followers of Lollius Urbicus for the peculiar kind of decoration now referred to. There is nothing here like a reflection from the banks of the Nile, as little from those of the Tiber ; and, excepting the really well executed Pegasus, which would be no disgrace to a Vexillarius of ordinary taste, even had he mounted guard for many a season on the steps of the Parthenon, we can see nothing in the design but the stamp of an original and self-taught genius. The winged horse and sea goat are often found together on the Roman British inscriptions. The semi-circular ornaments, something like Parthian shields, terminating in rosettes, or eagles' heads, are still more common. These last were, doubtless, mere arbitrary decorations; the two first must, however, have had their signification; what that signification was it is difficult to determine."

The inscription on this stone is of similar import to the three formerly mentioned. Instead, however, of having been raised by its vexillation only, we find it dedicated to the Emperor by the entire legion. A part of the legend will be observed near the top, the remainder within the interior border, some of the Imperial titles being omitted, evidently for want of room. The whole may be read thus :—

> To the Emperor Antoninus
> Augustus Pius—Father of his Country—
> The Second Legion (surnamed) Augusta
> (dedicate this) having executed 4270 paces.

In the Hunterian Museum there is another stone which might almost be called a fac-simile (Fig. No. 1, Plate II.), but no record has been kept of where it was discovered. It is here introduced on account of its resemblance to the preceding slab. The inscription comprises a few words :—

L E G	*LEGIO*	*The Second*
II	*SECUNDA*	*Legion Augusta*
AVG. F.	*AUGUSTA FECIT,*	*Executed*
P IIII CXI.	*PASSUS IIII CXI.*	4111 *Paces.*

While the Pegasus and sea goat appear on the tablets of the 2nd, the wild boar seems to have been the distinguishing feature on those of the 20th Legion. (See Fig. No. 1, Plate I.). It is present, at all events, on a tablet found at Duntocher, and presented to the University of Glasgow by Mr. John Hamilton, of Barns. Stuart says the stone had met with a good deal of rough usage. The inscription is as follows (see Fig. No. 2, Plate II.) :—

IMP. C.	*Imperatori Caesari*
T. AE. HADRIANO	*Tito Aelio Hadriano*
ANTONINO AVG	*Antonino Augusto*
PIO P.P. VEX . LEG	*Pio, Patri Patriae, Vexillatio Legionis*
XX VV F E C	*Vicesimae Valentis Victris Fesit*
P	*Passus*

Other and in some respects more important stones have been found in and near Duntocher fort, notably one found in the month of June, 1812, on the farm of Braidfield, about half a mile south-east from Duntocher Station, which Stuart considers to be the *chef d'œuvre*

of the military artists who handled the chisel. It is a
large slab of freestone, 42½ by 30 inches. (Fig. No. 4,
Plate II.). The inscription is to the effect that the 6th
Legion had erected 3240 paces of the wall, with the
usual dedication.

At Duntocher a small votive altar has been found. It
was discovered by Archibald Bulloch, son of the old
miller of Duntocher, in the year 1829, while cutting
drains in a marshy portion of the farm of Easter Dun-
tiglennan, about half a mile north from the line of the
wall, and in the vicinity of the fort. It was lying flat in
the earth about two feet below the surface. The finder
removed it from its hiding place, and put it upon the
eaves of his father's antique cottage, where it was seen
by the author of the "Caledonia Romana" in 1843.
The cottage has since been demolished, but the altar was
rescued, and fell into the possession of the late Mr. John
Buchanan, Glasgow. When first found the letters I.O.M
(which stand for Iovi Optimo Maximo—to Jove the best
greatest) were visible, and recognised by the minister of a
neighbouring parish, but they were obliterated by twenty
years' exposure to the weather.

In the year 1775 some curious subterranean chambers
were exposed in a field immediately to the north of
where the fort stood, and not far from the church
in the vicinity of Duntocher Bridge. Some labourers

were at that time engaged in turning over the ground when they came upon a large stone, which was found to cover the mouth of a circular vault, about 4½ feet deep and 10 feet in diameter. The walls and floor were of hewn stone, the roof of bricks, and what says a great deal both for the skill of the builder and the strength of the cement employed, this roof was not arched but perfectly flat. No one would venture to enter until a young man of the neighbourhood offered his services and was lowered through the opening. This adventurous individual was alive in 1844, but died the following year at the age of 96 years, and was tenant in Duntocher Mill for 64 years. On descending he found that the vault was connected with two other chambers of the same size and identical in appearance. The passage from one to the other was by a narrow opening or doorway, having a neatly-executed groove on either side for the admission of a sliding panel, by means of which the communication between them might be cut off, as is shown on the accompanying plan:—

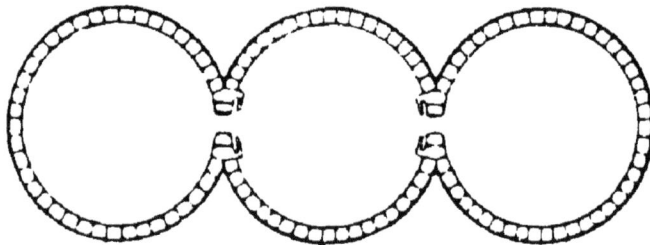

The only object of curiosity discovered within these vaults was an earthen jar standing in a niche of the wall, and containing a female figure, about 12 inches in height, formed of reddish clay. A few grains of wheat were likewise picked up, which renders it exceedingly probable that this subterranean building had been made use of as a granary. A drain for carrying off the water was found under the building. Bones of animals, and in particular the tusks apparently of boars, were found within the walls.

From Duntocher fort Gordon found the wall to be fairly visible for a quarter of a mile further east, passing to the left of a few houses called Cleddans and thence across a rivulet which goes by the same name. From it ascends a rising ground called Hutcheson Hill, on which the ditch is most visible, measuring about 33 feet in breadth and 8 or 10 feet in depth. From the rivulet called Cleddan Burn, he observes that the causeway takes a turn considerably southward from the ditch, keeping by the declivity or foot of the Hutcheson Hill, no doubt for the easier marching of the soldiers who travelled it.

In the spring of 1865 a legionary stone was found on the southern slope of the hill, at the depth of 3 feet below the surface. The slab measured 2 feet 10 inches by 2 feet 3 inches by 4 inches thick. (Fig. No. 3, Plate IV.). The inscription translated reads as follows;---

"To the Emperor Cæsar Titus Aelius Hadrianus
"Antoninus Augustus Pius, the Father of his Country,
"a vexillation of the 20th Legion, the valiant and
"victorious, constructed 3000 paces of the wall."

This stone was taken away to Chicago, U.S.A., where
all trace of it has been lost. A plaster cast is now in
the Hunterian Museum, from which the sketch has
been taken.

Gordon further says, "the vallum descends from the
above-mentioned hill to another brook called the burn of
the Peel Glen, at which place, where it crosses, the
foundation of a Roman bridge appears, consisting of large
square stones regularly cut and chequered, but most of
them are taken away for building the houses in the
neighbourhood, nor am I sure but that where the houses of
the Peel Glen are there might have been another fort, seeing
the foundations of stone buildings appear pretty visible
on this ground, though not so distinct as to afford me an
opportunity for taking their true dimensions and draught."

From this place a little further eastward the ditch
ascends a rising ground called Castlehill, where are to be
seen the vestiges of another castellum or fort upon the
wall. Here, on the Castlehill or third fort, a legionary
stone was discovered (Fig. 4, Plate III.), and in 1694
presented by Mr. Graham of Dougalston to the
University of Glasgow. The second stone found here

was a votive altar, the first we have met with along the
course of the wall, with the exception of the one referred
to as found at Duntocher. It is peculiarly interesting on
account of the dedication, and somewhat singular
combination of letters which it in some instances
exhibits. (Fig. No. 2, Plate III.). It was discovered in
1826 and presented to the Hunterian Museum by the
proprietor. It is rather above the average size, measuring
41 inches in height and 14 to 15 inches in breadth, and
the shape of the letters are exactly similar to those
which appear on the legionary inscriptions, showing it
to have belonged most probably to the second century.

The dedication reads as follows :—

> To the Eternal Field Dieties
> of Britain,
> Quintus Pisentius Justus,
> Praefect of The Fourth Cohort
> of the Gaulish Auxiliaries
> (dedicates this)
> His vow (being) most willingly fulfilled.

Another legionary stone (Fig. No. 3, Plate III.), was
in the spring of 1847 discovered near the Castlehill, and
also the square base of a broken pillar (Fig. No. 1,
Plate III.), and a tablet. Both were found lying on
their edge, which seemed to warrant the inference that
they were hid in the ground by the Romans on their
departure from the spot. Stuart remarks "One motive

for hiding them from the insults of the wild native after the soldiers left may be inferred from the circumstance that the Emperor Antoninus Pius, to whom the tablet is dedicated, was held in great veneration."

From the fort of Castlehill going eastward the vallum passes a little to the north of a place called the Mosshead of Ledcameroch, the causeway appearing again near the ditch, and both ascending the Cameroch Hill, the military way being about 18 paces south of the ditch on a parallel with it; both run down the higher ground to the village of New Kilpatrick, where, at one time, perhaps on the whole track of the wall from sea to sea, it is stated, the causeway could not be seen in greater perfection, measuring 20 feet in breadth.

The fort at New Kilpatrick was of an oblong form, rounded at the corners, the area enclosed measuring 480 by 330 feet. The military way passed directly through it, and its distance from the Castlehill was rather more than a mile and a third.

Two legionary stones were found here, and like those at Duntocher, shown on Plate II., Nos. 1 and 3, the one seems to be a copy of the other.

The first is a freestone slab, 5 feet long by 2½ broad, dedicated to the Emperor Antoninus Pius by the Vexillation of the Sixth Legion *Victrix* on their having completed 3665 paces of the wall. (See Fig. No. 1,

E

Plate IV.). The second stone (Fig. No. 2, Plate IV.), was found on the farm of Low Mullochan in the year 1803, a notice announcing the discovery, appearing in the *Glasgow Courier*, 5th March of that year.

See Appendix

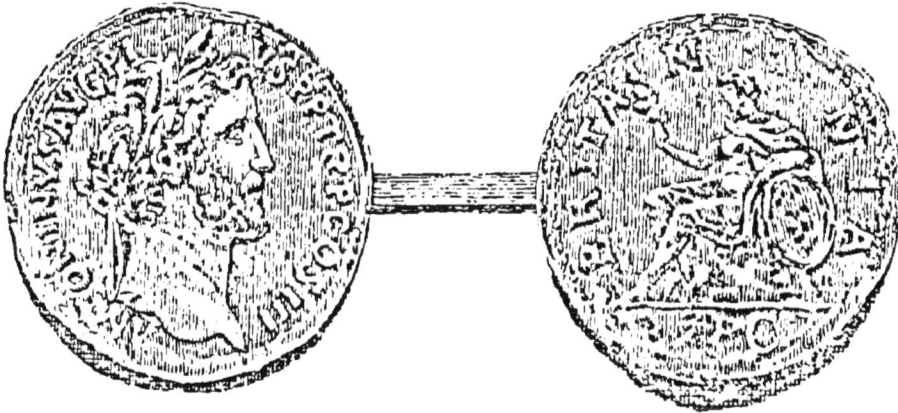

A COIN OF ANTONINUS.

CHAPTER IV.

ST. PATRICK.

THIS highly honoured and much revered saint—from whom the parish derives its name, and to whom the church was originally dedicated—is considered by the best authorities to have been born, if not at Kilpatrick at least in the vicinity, in the last quarter of the fourth century, whence he was carried off to Ireland, while yet a boy of 16 years, by Irish freebooters. There were at one time in the diocese of Glasgow six parishes deriving their name from St. Patrick, but we are told the most ancient and distinguished was Kilpatrick in the Lennox. Much controversy has arisen, and that for a long period, as to the birthplace of St. Patrick, Ireland and France having each their champions, Boulogne in the latter country claiming to be his natal place. As already mentioned the majority of critics now uphold the claim of Strathclyde. The Scotic freebooters from Antrim frequently ravaged the shores of the Firth of Clyde, and the Romans must have suffered much at their hands, as is evidenced by the numerous finds of Roman coins all along the Antrim coast. In the "Confession of St. Patrick,"* which, from the rude and ungrammatical character of its Latin, is a strong evidence of its genuineness, the writer says :—"I, Patrick, a sinner, the rudest and the least of all the faithful, and most contemptible to very many, had for my father Calpornius, a deacon, a son of Potitus, a presbyter, who dwelt in the village of Bannavem, Taberniae, for he had a small farm hard by the place where I was taken captive. I was then nearly 16 years of age. I did not know the true God, and I was taken to Ireland in captivity with so many thousand men, in accordance with our deserts, because we departed from God, and we kept not His precepts, and were not obedient to our priests who admonished us for our salvation." In his "Epistle to Coroticus" St. Patrick further says :—"I was a freeman according to the flesh. I was born of a father who was a Decurio; for I bartered my noble birth—I do not blush or regret it —for the benefit of others." Decurians formed what might be called local Town Councils in every small town and village about the year 400.

While called Patrick, or Patricius, which was a common name among the Romans of Britain, he had, as Tirechan informs us, no less than three Celtic names—Succetus (Sucat), Magonus, and Cothraige (Cothrighe).

---

* "The Writings of Patrick the Apostle of Ireland," by Rev. C. H. H. Wright, D.D., London, N.D.

Patrick's place of captivity was close to the village of Broughshare, five miles from Ballymena, in the valley of the Braid, near the Hill of Slemish. There is a townland in the valley still called Bally-lig-Patrick, the townland of Patrick's Hollow. Here is a cave built with remarkable strength; it has had at least three compartments, and one of them is supplied with air by a chimney. The river Braid, originally called Braghad, a gullet or windpipe, and used to signify a gorge or deeply cut glen, forms the boundary between the parishes of Racavan, or Rathcavan, on the south and Skerry on the north of the river. There are in the district the ruins of a cluster of ancient buildings, formerly surrounded by a deep ditch and parapet, and the adjoining locality is known in the county as St. Patrick's Chapel. Patrick was employed by a chieftain, Milchu by name, son of Hua Bain, King of North Dalriada, to feed cattle, and served him six years. Escaping from slavery he reached his home again, after having been, as some think, a second time in captivity. His own words are :—"And again, after a few years, I was in the Britains with my parents, who received me as a son, and earnestly besought me that now at least, after the many hardships I had endured, I would never leave them again. And there I saw indeed, in the bosom of the night, a man coming as it were from Ireland, Victoricus by name, with innumerable letters, and he gave one of them to me, and

I read the beginning of the letter containing "The voice of the Irish."

The result of this vision was that Patrick returned to Ireland to preach the Gospel, having, as he again says, given up his "noble birth for the benefit of others."

God blessed his labours in Ireland above measure: yet the modesty and humility exhibited by him in the account presented of his marvellous success is most remarkable. "There is, moreover," Dr. Wright says, "in his writings a display of genuine missionary spirit, which as it has roused many a Christian worker to action in the past, may well stir up many in our day also. Patrick everywhere displays an earnest trust and faith in the constant protection of a gracious Providence. His love for the souls of the men among whom he laboured, notwithstanding the ill-treatment he received at their hands, is remarkable. His honest simplicity and the contempt everywhere displayed for the riches of the world deserve far more general recognition than they have yet received. His acquaintance with the Holy Scripture, with the phraseology of which his Writings are thoroughly imbued, and his desire to conform his doctrine to their teaching, is significant. To him God and Satan, heaven and hell, were great realities: 'he endured as seeing Him who is invisible' (Heb. xi. 27)."

The genuine writings of Patrick are three in number, namely, "Patrick's Hymn," "His Confession," and "His Epistle to Coroticus"; the doubtful remains are the "Dicta Patricii," the "Proverbs of Patrick," and the "Interview of Patrick with the daughters of King Loegaire." There are some other works attributed to Patrick which have been condemned as spurious by competent scholars.

What is considered by the best authors to be St. Patrick's copy of the Gospels is one of the most treasured possessions of the Royal Irish Academy. It is enclosed in a shrine called the "Domnach Airgid." The shrine is an oblong box, nine inches by seven, and five inches in height. It is composed of three distinct covers, in the ages of which there is obviously a great difference. The inner or first cover is of wood, apparently of yew, and may be coeval with the manuscript it is intended to preserve. The second, which is of copper plated with silver, is assigned to a period between the sixth and twelfth centuries, from the style of its scroll or interlaced ornaments. The figures in relief and letters on the third cover, which is of silver plated with gold, leave no doubt of its being the work of the fourteenth century.

St. Patrick's bell is also preserved in Dublin. It is rudely made of hammered iron, rivetted, and coated with bronze. Its height is 7¾ inches, including the handle,

the width of the mouth 4⅞ by 3⅞ inches, and the
entire weight 3 lbs. 11 oz. The case or shrine in which
it is enclosed is of bronze, and richly ornamented in
gold and silver, and is supposed to have been made
between the years 1091 and 1105. The bell and shrine

St. Patrick's Bell

were in the custody of the family of Mulholland until the
year 1798, when it was gifted by the then holder, a
poor schoolmaster, Mulholland by name, to a former
pupil, Mr. M'Lean of Belfast. They are now among

the greatest treasures of the museum of the Royal Irish Academy*

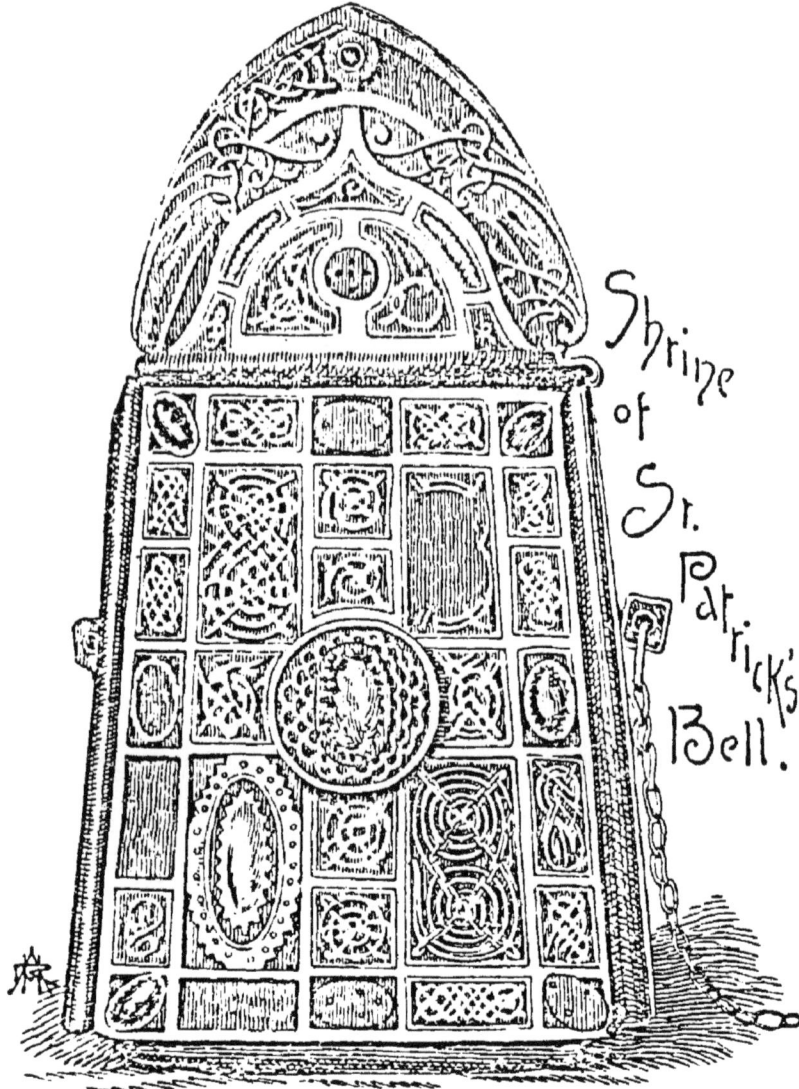

"The Hymn" is written in a very ancient dialect of Irish in the original, and the meaning of some of the

* Anderson's "Scotland in Early Christian Times," Edinburgh, 1881, page 203

words and phrases is uncertain. It is one of those
compositions termed by the Latin name of Lorica, or
"breastplate," the repetition of which was supposed to
guard a traveller like a breastplate from spiritual foes.
The first two verses of the "Hymn," or "Breastplate,"
read as follows :—

> I bind myself to-day
> To a strong power, an invocation of the Trinity.
> I believe in a Threeness, with confession of a Oneness,
> In the Creator of Judgment.

> I bind myself to-day
> To the power of the birth of Christ, with His baptism;
> To the power of the crucifixion, with His burial:
> To the power of His resurrection, with His ascension;
> To the power of His coming to the judgment of Doom.

The eleventh and last verse reads :—

> Salvation is the Lord's—
> Salvation is the Lord's—
> Salvation is Christ's:
> Let Thy salvation, O Lord, be ever with us.

This hymn has been set to music as a sacred cantata
by Sir Robert Stewart, Professor of Music, in the University of Dublin, and was performed for the first time in
St. Patrick's Cathedral, Dublin, on St. Patrick's Day,
March 17, 1888.

The dedications to St. Patrick in the locality are
numerous. In the castle of Dumbarton there was a
chapel dedicated to him from a very ancient date. Adam,

the chaplain of the castle, appears as a witness to a deed in 1271, and in the Exchequer Rolls of this period payments to the "capella sancti Patricii infra Castrum" frequently appear. Robert III., in 1390, granted this chapel 10 merks sterling yearly, out of the burrow mails of Dumbarton. The Parish Church of Dumbarton is sacred to his memory, as well as a collegiate church for a provost, and six prebendaries, which was founded by Isabel Dunbar, of Albany, and Countess of Lennox, in 1450, in the burgh town.

In Strathblane Parish there is "St. Patrick's Well," which used to be held sacred, and on the 1st of May, up to the beginning of this century, many a pilgrim drank its healing waters.

From the evidence led at a dispute about the lands of Kilpatrick, which will be referred to further on, there can be no doubt that, in the remote past, pilgrims came to worship at the shrine of St. Patrick in the village church, as the holder of the lands appears to have been under an obligation to receive and entertain those parties who came thither for that object. Duffgal, or Dougal, rector of the church about 1233, endowed the abbey with the land called Patrick's Seat, the locality of which it is now impossible to determine.

Besides the church dedicated to St. Patrick—which was said to be built on soil brought from Ireland in honour of its patron—we have St. Patrick's, or the Trees' Well, adjoining the church, which has been used until lately from time immemorial by the villagers, but now has been found unfit for use, and consequently ordered to be closed up. There is St. Patrick's Rock, near Erskine Ferry, on which, it is said, he was fishing as a boy when carried off to Ireland. Local tradition says erroneously, that St. Patrick was buried in his native place, but the Irish chroniclers tell us he lies buried in Downpatrick.

> "In Down three saints one tomb fill,
> Patrick, Bridget and Columkille."

CHAPTER V.

ECCLESIASTICAL HISTORY.

WHEN the Romans marched into Caledonia they found this part of the country peopled by a tribe whom they called the Damnonii or Damnii, a Cymric branch of the Celtic race. The district afterwards came to be called Cumbria or Strathclyde, the capital of which was Alcluith or Dumbarton. Under the civilising influence of the Romans, no doubt the inhabitants of this parish would, in their manners and customs, be far in advance of their wild neighbours the Picts, and that they were Christians we learn from St. Patrick's confession already referred to.

On the retiral of the Romans in the beginning of the 5th century, Strathclyde became a perfect battlefield. The Picts, Scots, and Saxons harassed the Britons; and latterly, the Danes in 870, under Ivan and Olave, having plundered Alcluith of all that was valuable, spread themselves over the surrounding country, and after twelve months' oppression, took their departure for Ireland. It was during these struggles that the great Cymric hero, Arthur the Faultless, King of the Poets, first saw the light.

Gildas in the 6th century, and Nennius in the 7th, relate
the real Arthur's history; while Merlin, the poet of Tweeds-
dale, and Llywarch Hen and Taliesin, both poets of the
Lennox, sing his praises. It has been thought that one
of the battles of Arthur was fought in the neighbourhood
of Duntocher, certainly in the neighbouring parish of
Strathblane, where "Arthur's stone" bears witness to one
of his victories.

About the year 900, Donald, the last of the Cymric or
Brython Kings, died, and was succeeded by Donald, a
brother of Constantine, King of the Scots. In 945,
King Eadmund, who the year previous had harried
all the Cumbrian kingdom, gave it all up to
Malcolm, King of the Scots, on the condition that he
should be his co-operator both on sea and land; and
though there seems to have continued a line of Strathclyde kings, they were certainly subservient to the King
of the Scots. Strathclyde was finally merged into Scotia
or Scotland in 1038, when Duncan succeeded his grand-
father Malcolm, son of Kenneth, as King of the united
Scottish, Pictish, and Cymric Thrones.

The earldom of Lennox, which was also known as the
Levanax or Leamhainach, derived its name from the
river Leven, the principal stream in the earldom,
so called from flowing through a forest of the
Leamhan or elm tree. The inhabitants were known as

into the possession of Aluin, or Allan, the first of the old
Earls of Lennox. The land tenure having become

SEAL OF THE ....

feudalised, the Earls of Lennox bestowed estates great
and small on the Church, and we now propose to give
an account of the liberal endowments made by them
to the Abbey of Paisley of the lands at their disposal
in the parish.

Deriving its name from St Patrick, the church had in

trious saint. Following the fashion of the times, the
church of Kilpatrick, which had been built on the supposed birthplace of the saint, with the lands granted
to it by the Earls of Lennox, was conveyed in
1227 by Maldowen, or Malcolm, the earl of the
time, to the Monastery of Paisley, to God, St. James,
St. Mirren, of Paisley, and for the soul of Alexander II.,
of himself, and all his race. "Lying on the northern
bank of the Clyde," Dr. Cameron Lees writes,* "they
formed a goodly possession, and probably on that account
were difficult to retain. The wild Highlandmen who
inhabited that part of the Lennox were continually seeking,
by fair means and by foul, to obtain possession of the
ground, and it took all the power of the Church to hold
its own against their devices. The family of Lennox
themselves seem no sooner to have parted with their fair
lands than they sought to get them back. The eldest
son of the Earl challenged the right of his father to
bestow certain of the lands which he said belonged to
him hereditarily, and the Abbot had to give him 60
merks to buy off his claim, or, as it is put, *pro bono
pacis*. Duffgal, or Dougal, the brother of Earl Maldowen,
made himself particularly obnoxious. He was at the
time of his brother's gift rector of the Church of
Kilpatrick, and probably thought the Abbot an intruder

* History of Paisley Abbey. 1878, page 60 *et seq.*

in his domains. Being a Churchman, and thus probably possessed of some skill in the drawing up of deeds, he forged charters, making himself out proprietor of the lands of Cochmanach, Dalevanach, Bachan, Fimbalach, Edenbernan, Drumcrew, Craigentalach, Monachkernan, Drumtechglenan, Cultebut and Losset, and entrenching himself behind these titles, he defied Abbot William and his convent to meddle with him. The Abbot, having found a former appeal to Rome successful, carried his grievance, June, 1232, to Pope Gregory IX., who issued a commission to his beloved sons the Deans of Cunningham and Carrick and the master of the School of Ayr to try the case between Duffgal and the Abbot. For a time the Kilpatrick rector kept to his own side of the river, and refused to answer the citations of the papal judges or to appear before them. At last, however, Duffgal's courage gave way before the threat of excommunication and consignment to the secular power, and in the Parish Church of Ayr, on the Sabbath following the Lord's Day on which is sung *Quasi modo geniti*, he appeared before the deputies. The charge was brought against him of having forged charters in order to obtain possession of certain lands contrary to his own salvation and the duty which he owed to the Church. Duffgal made no answer to this grave accusation, but, smitten by his own conscience, and seeing the imminent

F

danger to his body and soul if the charges were proved
against him, sought mercy instead of judgment, and
placed himself in the hands of the Abbot and convent,
who, on the advice of the judges, gave him the mercy
he sought, and allowed him to hold his church and a
caracute* of land at Cochmanach. Duffgal then made
a formal resignation of his lands, endowed the
Abbey with the land called Patrick's Seat,† and confessing
in the most abject manner his wicked forgery,
betook himself to his church and diminished acres,
probably thankful to have got off so well. It has been
said that the mass of evidence given by the large body
of witnesses called in this dispute is worthy of a more
advanced age, and the brief and retour of the inquest
concerning the succession of Duffgal of Lennox carries
back to the reign of Alexander II. a very peculiar form
of procedure, altogether without that connection with
church courts to which in general may be traced the
early introduction of legal technicalities in a remote and
otherwise barbarous country.

There were other lands in question before the judges
besides those wrongly held by the Rector of Kilpatrick,
and the name of one of them, that of Monachkernan, appears constantly in the charters, inhibitions,

---

* A caracute of land—108 acres.
† Dennistoun MSS.

and agreements of the times. Monachkeneran, Cultebuthe, Drumtechglenan, and other lands lying to the east of the Church of Kilpatrick had been tenanted in the end of the 12th or beginning of the 13th century by a person named Beda Ferdan, who lived in a large house built of twigs, "*Habitantem in quaddam domo, magna fabricata de virgis,*" * and who undertook for his holding the duty of receiving and feeding such pilgrims as came to the shrine of St. Patrick. A full account of this investigation is given in the Reg. de Passelet, from which we have drawn the narrative. The following are the names of some of the witnesses :—Anekol, Gilbethoc, Ressin, Nemias, Rotheric Beg, and Gillekonel Manthac. Beda Ferdan had not been allowed to retain peaceful possession of his lands, but had been slain in defence of the rights and liberty of the Church, and at the time of the Papal Commission which dispossessed the rector, Monachkeneran was held by a certain Gilbert, the son of Samuel of Renfrew, probably a follower of the house of Lennox, and Malcolm Begg had sold Cateconnen "prae timore." Dugald, the son of Cristinus, a former judge of Lennox, vindicated his right to the possession of Cultebuthe on the Clyde, and to a small piece of land which lay between the Church and the river on the east. †   With Gilbert, therefore, the

---

* Reg. de Pas., p. 166.
† Crawford's "History of Paisley, 1782," fol. 59-60

Papal judges proceeded to deal, and summoned him to
appear before them in the Parish Church of Irvine on
the Monday preceding St. Matthews anniversary, 1233.*
Gilbert treated their citation very lightly, and merely
sent them word that he would do what was right, taking
no further notice of their summons. They proceeded,
therefore, in his absence, to take proof, and to hear
the witnesses brought forward by the convent. The
evidence of these witnesses is taken in a manner that
would do credit to any Court of Justice, and what
they said is set down in a very terse and distinct
style. Two diets of proof were held, and fourteen witnesses sworn and examined, all of whom testified to the
lands in question having belonged to the Church of Kilpatrick. Some having been born and brought
up in the neighbourhood remembered Beda Ferdan well;
one, Alexander, son of Hugh, stated that when he was a
boy, more than 60 years before, he and his father had been
entertained as strangers by him; another, Anekol by name,
swore that when Earl David of Lennox, in the time of
King William, sought to raise men from the lands of
Kilpatrick as from the other lands of his barony, the
Church interfered in defence of her tenants, and proved
their exemption from military service; Thomas Gaskel
deponed to the same effect, and added that he afterwards

saw Cristinus, son of Beda, possessing these lands by
the same title as his father, and that the whole territory
of the Church of Kilpatrick was divided into four parts,
of which one was possessed by Beda Ferdan and the
other three by others, who also in the name of the Church
administered to such as chanced to come that way. The
judges held that the Abbot and convent had amply
proved their right to the lands in dispute, according
to their own judgment, and that of men skilled both
in canonical and civil law. They allowed them possession, and condemned Gilbert in expenses, namely, 'in
thirty pounds to be sworn to and taxed.' They then
asked execution of their sentence of the Bishop of
Glasgow. Gilbert was excommunicated for contumacy,
and King Alexander II. at the request of the Com-
missioners put in force against him the secular power.
This does not, however, appear to have been done with
sufficient energy, for sometime afterwards, we find they
again had recourse to His Majesty, wishing him 'salvation in that which gives salvation to kings,' and
asking him not to relax his efforts till the excommunicated Gilbert had obeyed the sentence and
satisfied his judges. Neither the secular nor the
sacred power appear to have been able, however,
to dispossess him, and it was not until two
years afterwards that his chief, the Earl, induced

him to resign his charters and the claim to his lands, by agreeing to pay him sixty merks of silver, in three portions of twenty merks at a time.

In 1250 the Earl repeated a general confirmation of all their lands within the Earldom, adding the right of pasturage formerly liferented by Ralph, the Chaplain Royal, to the north of Baccan, by the valley which slopes northward from Lochbeth to the waters of Corenade, thence westward along that water to the brook which flows northward from Salvari, where the men of his brother Dugald formerly had shielings, and thence to the march of Fimbelach.

From the great Bull of Pope Clement IV., 1265, we learn of the whole of the lands and churches owned by the Abbey of Paisley, and among them those in the County of Lennox, "which are commonly called Coupinanach, Edin-bernan, Bacchan, Finbelach, Cragbrectalach, Druncrene, Dallenneach, Drumtocher, Drumteyglenan, Drumdeynains, Cultbuy and Renfoyd : and the lands which they had had in the place called Monachkenran, with its pertinents." When Drumtocher and Duntiglenan were conveyed to the abbey by Earl Maldowen, they were burdened with the life rent of Ralph, Chaplain Royal, but he transferred to the abbey the annual payment due by the said Ralph of three silver merks, one chalder meal, and one chalder malt.*

---

* Dennistoun MSS.

The title of the abbey to the valuable lands in Kilpatrick, which had been disputed in the time of Abbot William, was again called in question. That energetic cleric had apparently brought all the matters in dispute to a satisfactory termination, but when his guiding hand was removed the old difficulties began afresh. So early as 1272, three persons—John de Wardroba, Bernard de Erth, or Airth, and Norinus de Monnorgund—who had married grand nieces and heiresses of Dugald, the contumacious rector whom Abbot William had so summarily silenced, renewed in right of their wives, the claim that he had abandoned, and were apparently inclined to prosecute it with vigour. A jury met at Dumbarton on Friday, before the feast of St. Dunstan Archbishop (15th May), and found that Maria, Elena and Forveleth, daughters of the late Finlay of Campsie, were the true lawful heirs of the deceased Dugald, brother of Maldown, 3rd Earl of Lennox. The writ from Alexander III. to the Sheriff of Dumbarton is dated 24th April, 1271. The Abbot did not, however, go to law with them. Possibly there may have been dealings with Dugald that it would not have been convenient to bring to light. The claim was hushed up, and the claimants bought off by the payment on the part of the Abbot of 150 merks, "*pro bono pacis*," after which he received from each of them a separate resignation of all their claims, and in 1273 the Earl of

Lennox, when he received knighthood, wishing to be
at peace with the Church before undergoing that ceremony,
confirmed to the monastery all the lands which they held
in his barony, and added a plenary exemption to the
inhabitants of the territory from all subsidies and extor-
tions. But in the time of the Abbot Walter, the old
disputes broke out again. Taking advantage of the
troubled state of Scotland, vigorous attempts were made
in 1294 to strip the abbey of its Dumbartonshire
possessions. They might have succeeded had not
Walter found a firm friend and ally in his diocesan,
Robert Wishart, the friend both of Wallace and of Bruce,
and the determined foe of England, who entered into
the contest between the abbey and its assailants with the
vigour which history shows characterised all his actions,
and who hurled against them the thunders of the
Church. A certain Robert Reddehow, and Johanna, his
wife, claimants like those already noticed, brought the
abbot into the Court of the Earl of Lennox, who
with his bailiff, under Royal Authority, proceeded to
try the case, as his predecessor had done with the
claimants of his time. The abbot, instead of giving
these claimants a sum of money "*pro bono pacis*," refused
to meet them in a secular court, or to acknowledge the
right of the Earl, and those holding court with him,
to interfere with the property of the Church, even

under Royal Authority. The bishop, with whom the
"Royal Authority" of John Baliol did not probably count
for much, at once took the same view, and stood on the
high ground of "spiritual independence." He issued a
mandate requiring the Earl wholly to cease from the
cognition of such causes as by Royal Authority he had
caused to be dragged into his court, and ordered
Reddehow and his wife to desist from their prosecution
of the abbot under pain of the greater excommunication.
The Earl and his bailiff disregarded these fulminations,
and proceeded in his Court "against God and justice,
and to the great prejudice of ecclesiastical liberty" to
cognose upon the lands in dispute. Robert Reddehow
and his wife, Johanna, fearless of the "greater excommunication," also persisted in litigation, maintaining a protracted
obduracy of mind, and irreverently contemning as sons
of perdition the Keys of the Church. This was more
than the bishop could endure, and he laid injunctions on
five of his clergy—the Vicars of Cathcart, Pollok, Car-
munnoc, Kilbarchan, and Kilmalcolm—to go, on the day
on which the abbot was summoned to the Earl's Court,
to the place of trial, and, taking with them "six or seven
of their order, personally to advance to the said Earl, his
baillies, and those holding court with them, and again
warn them altogether to desist from the cognition of all
such causes." He further enjoined them again to warn

Reddhow and his wife by name, and any others who
might prosecute the said religious men in regard to their
lands before said Court, wholly to cease from their
prosecution. Should all this fail, the guilty parties were
to be held as excommunicated, and their lands and
chapels interdicted. The vicars, clothed in white sacerdotal
vestments, in full Court, were further, if they thought ex-
pedient, publicly and by name, to denounce and cause
to be denounced, the persons thus excommunicated in
all the churches of the Deanery of Lennox, and Arch-
deanery of Glasgow, especially on each Lord's day and
festal day, with candles burning and bells ringing, after
offering of masses. They were to warn all the faithful in
Christ to avoid them, and to place the lands and chapels
of such as refused to obey under special interdict. The
inhibition expressly warns Sir Patrick de Graham, Duncan,
the son of Ameledy, Maurice, of Ardcapell, and twenty-
four others, not to presume to intercommune with the
excommunicated persons, or any one of them, in Court
or out of Court, by assistance, favour, or counsel, by
supplying them with food, drink, or fire, by grinding
corn, or buying and selling. This terrible document is
dated from Casteltaris, or Carstairs, 22nd August, 1294.
Whether it had altogether the desired effect is doubtful,
for we find the bishop two years afterwards returning to
the contest, and commanding the Dean of the Christian

Jurisdiction of the Lennox to take with him four or five
of his Order, and admonish the Earl and his bailiffs not
to presume to drag the Abbot and Convent of Paisley
before his Court in regard to the oft-disputed lands. The
whole controversy furnishes a striking illustration of the
struggle between the spiritual, or rather ecclesiastical, and
secular powers, which, in some form or other, is constantly taking place even in modern times. *

The monks of Paisley, in common with other Scots
ecclesiastics in those times, took the patriotic side. They
were the good friends of Robert Wishart, the Bishop of
Glasgow, who was so great a patriot that no oath could
possibly bind him in allegiance to the English King, and
who passed a great many years in an English prison.
That the church lands of Kilpatrick furnished men who
fought under the Earl of Lennox at Bannockburn is
evident from the fact that in 1318 Malcolm, Earl of
Lennox, admitted that the contingent furnished by the
Abbot from the Kilpatrick lands was of free grace and
favour.

The learned antiquary, George Chalmers, has justly
observed that the Bruce won his crown mainly through
the patriotism of the clergy, coupled with the devotion
of the common people.

A charitable concession, which must have been

* Hist of Paisley Abbey. page 166. *et seq.*

gratifying to the Abbot John and his brethren in their low
estate (the Abbey having been burned in 1307 by the
English), was made by Earl Malcolm of Lennox, 1329.
He gave them all their lands in his country of Dumbartonshire. The contested properties of Monachkeneran,
Bachan, and others, appear in his charters for the last
time, all their rights, churches, and fishings being for
ever secured, so that no person, clerical or lay, should
interfere with them again. These properties had been an
incessant cause of disquietude during nearly a century,
and many of them, amid the confusion of the War of
Independence, had in every likelihood been lost altogether. The Earl now confirmed them inalienably to the
Monastery 'for the soul of the illustrious King Robert of
Scotland,' who had died two years previously. In order
that the Convent might hold their lands with a firm hand,
he gave them power to have 'courts of life and mem-
bers,' and escheat at the death of a man, in all their
lands. These powers would enable them to keep all the
wild Celts on their Dumbartonshire lands thoroughly in
order, without help as formerly from the Bishop, of
spiritual excommunication. For the latter, the rude
marauders of the Lennox, as we have seen, cared but
little, and the Bishop thundered at them in vain ; but
the fear of execution and a short shrift could not fail to
instil into them wholesome respect for their monastic

superiors. The Earl, however, provided that when any were condemned to death, they should pay the penalty at his own gallows of Lennox.

In 1380, King Robert II. gave Abbot John a token of his goodwill by erecting into a barony all the Abbey lands of Lennox, with all the privileges which a barony usually possessed, assigning as the reason for this favour, that the Monastery had been founded by Walter, son of Alan Stewart of Scotland, of beloved memory, and liberally endowed by him and other of his ancestors, as well as by various other faithful Christians. In return for his concessions, the King asks the offering of their earnest prayers, and the only condition which he attaches to it is that they should continue to pay, as hitherto, five chalders of oatmeal to the watchmen of the Castle of Dumbarton. He reserved 'the four points of the Crown.'

To Abbot Tervas King James II. confirmed, in 1451, the regality into which Robert III. had erected the Abbey lands, granting even, in their Dumbartonshire lands, the four points of the Crown which that King had reserved—rape, rapine, murder and fire-raising.

Abbot Shaw, A.D 1478, like most of his predecessors, had to guard the possessions of his monastery against encroachments of various kinds. A certain Sir Hugh Fleming, of Dalnotter, gave him trouble about the pasturage lying between Bachan in Kilpatrick and his own property, Kynmunchayr. The Dean of Lennox was instructed by apostolic authority to assume with him chaplains and clerks, and going personally to the place of the king at Dumbarton, once, twice, and thrice, solemnly to warn Hugh, on the part of the Pope and the bishops of the Scottish church, that he was not under pain of excommunication, to draw the Abbot and convent before any lay tribunal, and to cite him to appear before apostolic delegates for the trial of his case. After this we hear no more of Hugh Fleming, who likely thought he would gain little by an appearance against the clergy in an ecclesiastical tribunal.

In the year 1275 an ecclesiastic, who is called Bagemont in the history and in the law of Scotland, but whose real name was Bayamond, came from the Pope to collect the tenth of all the benefices in North Britain, for the relief of the Holy Land. The clergy felt the oppression of paying truly one tenth of their real incomes, and induced Bayamond to repair to Rome in order to solicit some abatement of that burdensome imposition. The journey was unsuccessful, and Bayamond returned into Scotland, where he could not collect the tax, but found a grave.

In his tax-roll the value of the Kilpatrick vicarage is given at £53 6s. 8d., and it bears the same value in the books of the Collector-General of thirds of benefices, A.D. 1561 ; it also produced 28 chalders, 15 bolls, 2 firlots meal, and 7 chalders, 3 bolls, and 3 firlots barley.

In 1227, or before that date rather, when the Earl of Lennox, granted the church and lands to the Abbey, the vicarage was taxed at 12 merks of the altarage, or of the tithe of corn if the altarage was not sufficient. The procurations due the bishop of the diocese were taxed at one reception (*hospitum*) yearly.

CHAPTER VI.

THE ABBEY RENTAL BOOK.

MUCH valuable information regarding the Abbey lands in the parish is contained in the Rental Book, or Book of Leases, which was begun in the time of Abbot Crichton, A.D. 1460 and, continued by his successors. Dr. Cameron Lees, whom we again quote freely, says—" It is beautifully written and neatly kept, and perhaps, more than any other manuscript of this same kind that has been published, gives us an idea of the conduct of the monks in their capacity as landlords. The view one takes of their government, after a study of this volume, is a very kindly one, and corroborates all that historians tell us regarding the lands of those ecclessiastics being the best cultivated and the best managed in Scotland. There were good reasons why they should be so. The monks were not needy landlords, grinding out of their tenants every penny they were able to pay. They were proprietors whose own wants were few, and who had education enabling them to adopt the best methods of agriculture, and sense to encourage improvements. The tenants were exempt from military service. The husbandman

Milton Keynes UK
Ingram Content Group UK Ltd.
UKHW051328011024
1947UKWH00027B/156

9 781241 311056